Table of Contents

A Starfish Book

Teaching Tips for Caregivers:

As a caregiver, you can help your child succeed in school by giving them a strong foundation in language and literacy skills and a desire to learn to read.

This book helps children grow by letting them practice reading skills.

Reading for pleasure and interest will help your child to develop reading skills and will give your child the opportunity to practice these skills in meaningful ways.

- Encourage your child to read on her own at home
- Encourage your child to practice reading aloud
- Encourage activities that require reading
- Establish a reading time
- Talk with your child
- Give your child writing materials

Teaching Tips for Teachers:

Research shows that one of the best ways for students to learn a new topic is to read about it.

Before Reading

- Read the "Words to Know" and discuss the meaning of each word.
- Read the back cover to see what the book is about.

During Reading

- When a student gets to a word that is unknown, ask them to look at the rest of the sentence to find clues to help with the meaning of the unknown word.
- Ask the student to write down any pages of the book that were confusing to them.

After Reading

- Discuss the main idea of the book.
- Ask students to give one detail that they learned in the book by showing a text dependent answer from the book.

Christmas in

Italy

BUON NATALE

Many people celebrate Christmas in Italy.

The *piazza*, or town center, has a huge tree.

Houses also have trees and decorations.

Nativities tell the Christmas story.

Baby Jesus is put in the crib on December 24th.

Fun Fact:
Regular people and objects can be part of the nativity.

Children sing **carols** at different houses.

They pretend to be **shepherds**.

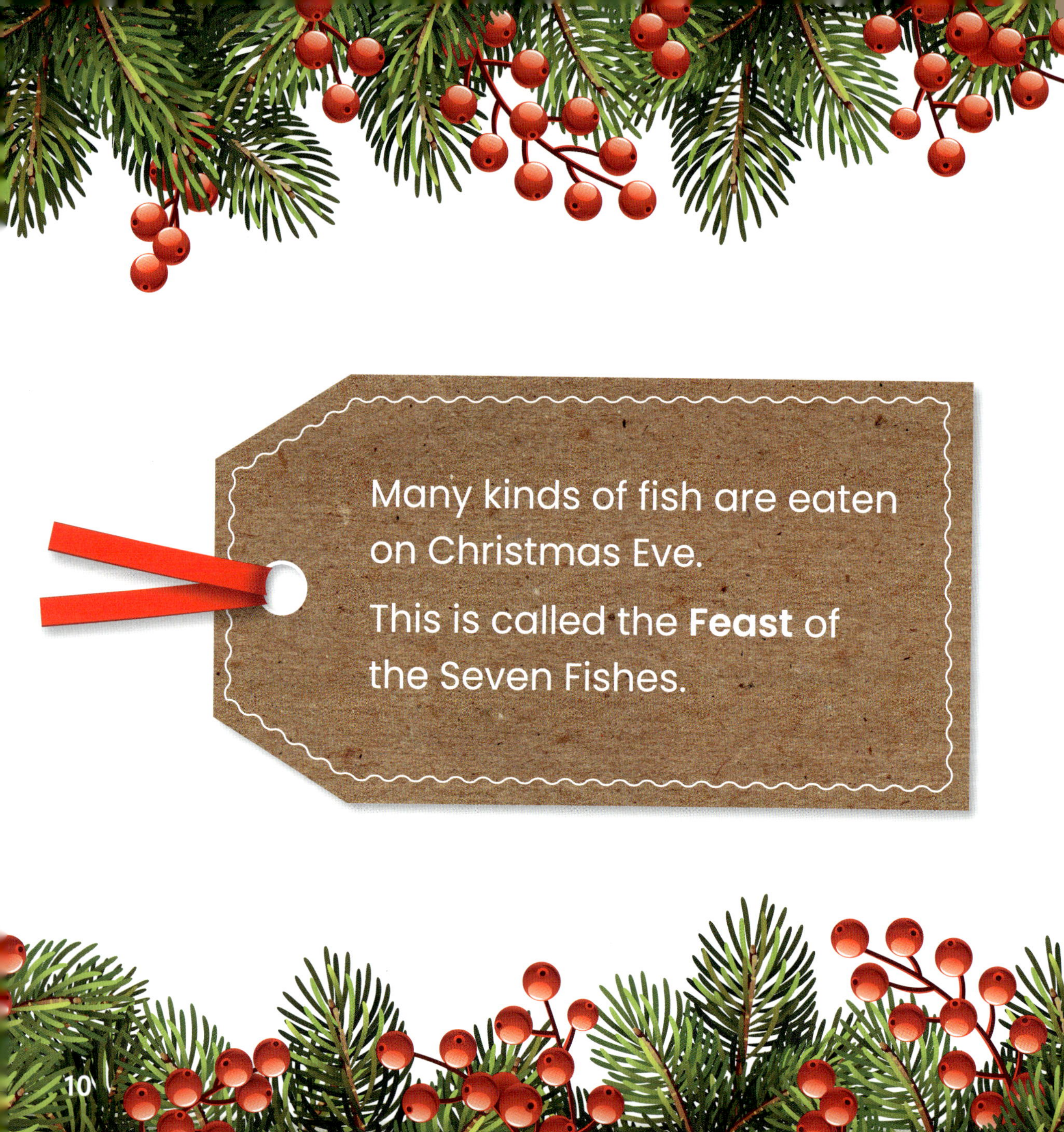

Many kinds of fish are eaten on Christmas Eve.

This is called the **Feast** of the Seven Fishes.

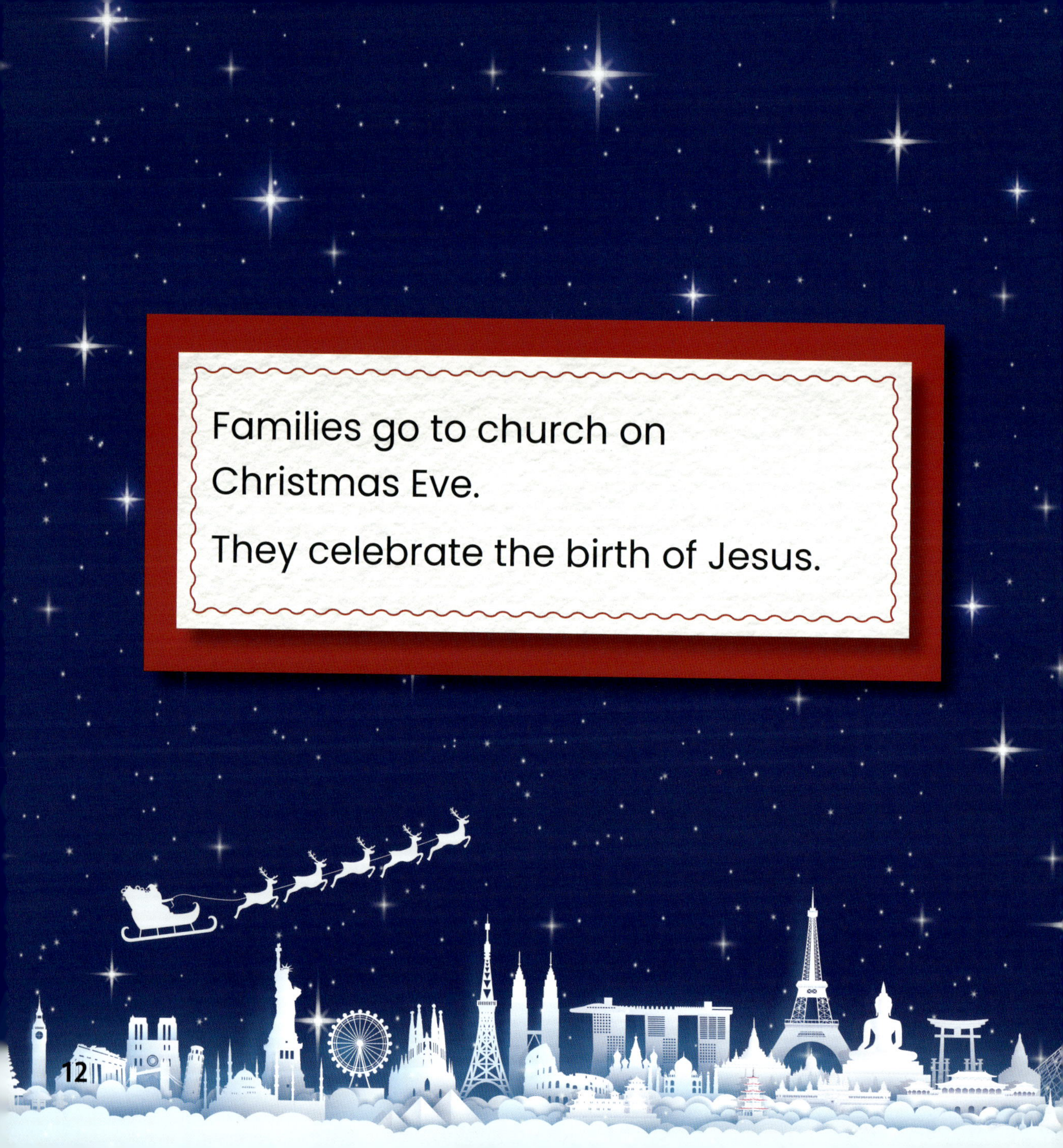

Families go to church on Christmas Eve.

They celebrate the birth of Jesus.

Fun Fact:
After church, some people ski down slopes at midnight on Christmas Eve.

A big lunch is eaten on Christmas Day.

There are many pasta dishes.

Struffoli, a sticky fried dough, is for dessert.

Santa Claus is called *Babbo Natale*.

He gives gifts on Christmas Day.

Children hang **stockings** on January 5th.

La Befana fills them with gifts.

She is like a witch.

Buona Befana
Fun Fact:
La Befana flies on a broomstick.

Craft: La Befana Broomstick

Materials

- burlap fabric
- scissors
- wooden dowel that is about 12 inches (30 centimeters) long and ¼ inch to ½ inch (½ to 1¼ centimeters) in diameter
- masking tape
- ribbon

Steps

1. Cut a rectangle of burlap about 10 inches (25 centimeters) wide and 6 inches (15 centimeters) long.
2. Unravel the burlap from one long edge to make bristles. Leave about 2 inches (5 centimeters) at the top unraveled.
3. Wrap the burlap lengthwise around the bottom of the dowel. The end of the dowel should be hidden.
4. Use the masking tape to secure the top of the burlap around the dowel.
5. Tie the ribbon around the top of the burlap to cover the tape.

Recipe: Struffoli (Honey Glazed Fried Dough Balls)

Ingredients

Balls:

- 1 cup flour
- 1 lemon, zested
- 1 orange, zested
- 1½ tablespoons sugar
- ¼ teaspoon salt
- ¼ teaspoon baking powder
- 2 ounces unsalted butter
- 2 medium eggs
- ⅓ teaspoon vanilla extract
- vegetable oil or canola oil for frying

Glaze:

- ½ cup honey
- ¼ cup white sugar
- ½ tablespoon lemon juice
- sprinkles
- candied fruits
- confectioners' sugar (powdered sugar)

Steps

Balls:

1. In a medium bowl, mix the flour, lemon zest, orange zest, sugar, salt, and baking powder.
2. In a food processor, mix the dry ingredients with the butter. Blend until it is the consistency of coarse cornmeal.
3. Add the eggs and vanilla extract. Blend until the dough becomes a ball.
4. Cover the dough with plastic wrap. Chill in the refrigerator for a minimum of 30 minutes.
5. Roll the dough into thick ropes about ¼-inch (½-centimeter) thick.
6. Cut the dough into ½-inch (1¼-centimeter) portions. Roll into tiny balls and lightly dust with flour.
7. In a saucepan, heat oil until it is 375° F (190° C). Meanwhile, line a large baking sheet or serving plate with paper towels.
8. Gently drop batches of dough into the oil. Fry until light golden brown (2 to 3 minutes).
9. Scoop out and let dry on the paper towels.

Glaze:

1. In a large saucepan, combine the honey, white sugar, and lemon juice. Cook on medium heat until the sugar is dissolved. Stir frequently.
2. Turn off the heat and remove from stove. Add the fried dough balls carefully to the mixture. Stir gently.
3. Once all the balls are covered, place on a serving platter. Set the remaining glaze aside.
4. Arrange the dough balls on the platter in a wreath shape or create a mountain of balls.
5. Pour the remaining glaze over the fried dough balls. Cover immediately with sprinkles, candied fruits, confectioners' sugar, or other edible decorations.

Words to Know

carols (KAR-uhlz): traditional, joyful songs, especially those sung at Christmas

feast (feest): a large, special meal

nativities (nuh-TIV-i-tees): stable scenes that show baby Jesus, Mary, Joseph, animals, shepherds, and angels

shepherds (SHEP-urdz): people who take care of sheep; in the Christmas story, an angel told shepherds about baby Jesus

slopes (slohps): areas of land on a mountain that are used for skiing

stockings (STAH-kingz): socks; at Christmas, large stockings are hung up to be filled with gifts

Index

Comprehension Questions

1. Families eat _____ types of fish on Christmas Eve.
   a. only a few
   b. many
   c. ten

2. La Befana is
   a. Santa Claus.
   b. Saint Nicholas.
   c. a witch.

3. Nativities tell the story of
   a. La Befana.
   b. Christmas.
   c. Babbo Natale.

4. True or false: People ski down mountains on Christmas Eve.

5. True or false: A small lunch is eaten on Christmas Day.

Answers
1. b 2. c 3. b 4. True 5. False

About the Author

Christina Earley lives in South Florida with her with husband, son, and dog named Bailey. Her favorite holiday is Christmas because it is a magical time of year. She collects ornaments that remind her of special places and events. She and her family have lots of fun baking cookies and eating candy canes while looking at Christmas lights.

Written by: Christina Earley
Design by: Jen Bowers
Editor: Kim Thompson

Photographs: Cover ©2015 Bucchi Francesco/Shutterstock/Shutterstock, pine ©Pasko Maksim/Shutterstock,world skyline©Painterstock/Shutterstock, background©ghenadie/Shutterstock, earth ©leonello/iStock; p.1 ©Mariana Mast/Shutterstock; p.3 ©2014 Veronica Louro/Shutterstock; p.5 ©2018 Arcansel/Shutterstock; p.7 ©2019 Di Gregorio Giulio/Shutterstock, ornament©ekler/Shutterstock; p.9 ©2013 Rob Hyrons/Shutterstock; p.11 ©2018 Brent Hofacker/Shutterstock; p.13 ©2017 Gekkon/Shutterstock; p.15 ©2020 Vincenzo De Bernardo/Shutterstock; p.16 ©2017 Tijana Moraca/Shutterstock; p.19 ©NGvozdeva/Shutterstock; p.20 ©2015 Seregam/Shutterstock

Library of Congress PCN Data
Christmas in Italy / Earley
Christmas Around the World
ISBN 978-1-63897-443-7 (hard cover)
ISBN 978-1-63897-558-8 (paperback)
ISBN 978-1-63897-673-8 (EPUB)
ISBN 978-1-63897-788-9 (eBook)
Library of Congress Control Number: 2022930312

Printed in the United States of America.

Seahorse Publishing Company
www.seahorsepub.com

Published in the United States
Seahorse Publishing
PO Box 771325
Coral Springs, FL 33077

Christmas is a special holiday that is celebrated all over the world. Look inside to learn the customs and traditions of people in Italy. Create a special Christmas craft and make a tasty recipe, too!

Books in the series *Christmas Around the World* include:

GRL: I

US: $8.75 CA: $9.75

ISBN 978-1-63897-558-8

50875

9 781638 975588

IL: K-2

SEAHORSE PUBLISHING
www.seahorsepub.com

Christmas
Around the World
Christmas in
Mexico
By Christina Earley
Starfish